THE DOG WHO THOUGHT HIS NAME WAS NO

D0434350

Tales of truth
to transform
your thinking

Judy Moore

CWR

Copyright © Judy Moore, 2017
Published 2017 by CWR, Waverley Abbey House, Waverley Lane, Farnham,
Surrey GU9 8EP, UK.
Reprinted 2018.
CWR is a Registered Charity – Number 294387 and a Limited
Company registered in England – Registration Number 1990308.
The right of Judy Moore to be identified as the author of this work has been
asserted by her in accordance with the Copyright, Designs and Patents Act 1988.
All rights reserved. No part of this publication may be reproduced, stored in
a retrieval system or transmitted, in any form or by any means, electronic,
mechanical, photocopying, recording or otherwise, without the prior permission
of CWR in writing.
For a list of National Distributors, see www.cwr.org.uk/distributors
Scripture references are taken from the Holy Bible, New International Version
(NIV) Anglicised, Copyright 1979, 1984, 2011 by Biblica, Inc.
Other versions are marked: *The Message*, Copyright 1993, 1994, 1995, 1996,
2000, 2001, 2002 by Eugene H. Peterson; Good News Translation (GNT),
Copyright 1992 by American Bible Society; English Standard Version (ESVUK),
Copyright 2001 by Crossway Bibles, a division of Good News Publishers; New
Living Translation (NLT), Copyright 1996, 2004, 2015 by Tyndale House
Foundation.Concept development, editing, design and production by CWR.
Every effort has been made to ensure that this book contains the correct
permissions and references, but if anything has been inadvertently overlooked
the Publisher will be pleased to make the necessary arrangements at the first
opportunity. Please contact the Publisher directly.
Cover image: CWR
Printed by Linney
ISBN: 978-1-78259-751-3

For my dad, Richard Moore and my sister,
Carol Fullbrook, who have shown me the 'yes'
of God's unconditional love.

In loving memory of my mum, Mavis Moore,
who taught us all how to tell a good story,
to love well and to laugh!

Contents

Foreword

We Christians are funny about the Bible. We will argue loudly and stubbornly about the exact meaning of some passage or other, possibly because having a fixed view is better than having no view at all, but we bypass or ignore general principles that others might consider blindingly obvious. The telling of stories is a good example. If there is one thing we know for sure, it is that Jesus did the vast majority of His teaching through stories or 'parables'. Anyone who has written using this medium, will be well aware of its two essential attributes.

First, to ensure that the stories sing with authenticity, they need to be based on personal memories or actual events. I have no idea if Jesus made written notes of His experiences and encounters in the years before His public ministry began, but I am absolutely sure that His fictional communications grew from that very fertile soil. I read it. I can feel it in my bones. I value it beyond most things, because, although separated by 2,000 years and nothing at all, He and I have a shared profession. We both work hard to captivate, enthuse and mobilise the hearts of those who listen and read. Granted, His creative works may have touched a few more hearts than mine but that doesn't matter; I enjoy the bond, however slender.

Some people are continuing the honourable tradition of storytelling, and Judy Moore is one of them. Judy has been my friend for a number of years, and I would like to tell you about some aspects of her character that feed into the speaking and writing that she does so extraordinarily well. Judy would laugh if I said that she is perfect – mainly because she is not, but she does embody a generosity of spirit that attracts and relaxes the folk she encounters. There are no unimportant people in the world as far as she is concerned. She sprinkles love around, a very necessary talent for storytellers.

The second attribute is that Judy tells stories remarkably well, both verbally and, somewhat to her own surprise, in written form. There are quite a lot of people around who write well and a few who have mastered the spoken word. Few are highly proficient in both. Shockingly, her stories are actually true. Imagine that! A storyteller who talks about things that have really happened. Not only that, but she manages to make a related and useful point from her personal experiences.

My friend Judy is an amazing woman of God. Like Jesus encountering the widow of Nain whose only son had died, Judy's heart goes out to those who are yearning to find a shepherd who will lead them with wisdom, humour and care. By being herself and by using her talent with words, Judy guides them gently to the master. I love her book, and I think you will as well.

Adrian Plass

Introduction

It may be a fable or an apocryphal tale, but there is a moving story of a dog who thinks his name is No. He hears the word so many times in his direction that he starts to answer to it as his name.

Names in the Bible are very significant. In some cases, people are given new names at a key moment in their life. Simon becomes Peter, and Saul becomes Paul. Our names are bound up in who we are and who we become. What we hear directed at ourselves begins to shape our identity, and can become the lens through which we view the world and ourselves. *The Dog Who Thought His Name Was No* can relate to all of us. There may be 'no's that we have heard and believed about ourselves. Have you been bullied and so believe that you are stupid or irritating? Have you been abused and led to believe that you are worthless and weak? Are you struggling with physical or mental illness and don't understand why God would allow it? Have you experienced failure and lost your sense of potential for the future? Have you lived your life seeking the approval of others because you never quite believe you're worthy of it? Have you lived so long with comparison and criticism that you have no sense of who you are?

My aim, in writing this book, is to unlock biblical truths using stories from my life. Stories full of both comedy and pathos. Biblical truths, when lovingly spoken in our direction, will shape our identity and change the way we view ourselves within God's world. Whether or not you know God and how He views you, I hope this book will show you that God has a place for you in His story and wants to give you a new identity – your true identity – lovingly made in the image of God.

Over the years, I have trained and worked as an actress, taught in a secondary school and am now part of the leadership team in a church. I have been fortunate enough to travel across our amazing world and experience times of absolute joy, but like many, have also known deep sorrow and loss. In relating stories from my past, I would like to share with you how God has used these experiences to teach me more about His character.

Stories have always been how I learn and understand the Christian faith. They always fascinate me, teach me, and entertain me. We all have a story to live out and a song to sing. Jesus has chosen us, called us and equipped us to play an amazing part in His story. Whether or not we believe in Him, Jesus knows us by name. He knows how many hairs are on our head and how many days will make up our life. He hasn't called us to be weird, fanatical or religious, He has called us into a relationship, into friendship. He is waiting for a response from every single one of us.

The dog who thought his name was No saw his identity in the negative. Let us continue to discover that God always has and always will see us in the positive. The 'no's we have believed can start to be replaced with His incredible truth. As you read this book, my hope and prayer is that you would hear God's resounding 'yes!' to you. 'Yes' – you are loved, 'yes' – He has made you and 'yes' – He wants you to be free to live out His teachings of love and compassion.

The following verses from 2 Corinthians reminds us what a positive and affirming God we have:

'Whatever God has promised gets stamped with the Yes of Jesus. In him, this is what we preach and pray, the great Amen, God's Yes and our Yes together, gloriously evident. God affirms us, making us a sure thing in Christ, putting his Yes within us. By his Spirit he has stamped us with his eternal pledge—a sure beginning of what he is destined to complete.' 2 Corinthians 1:20-22 (The Message)

ONE

SAMARITAN
OR SAMURAI
IN SUBURBIA?

At Christmastime last year, my dad reached that season of life when he needed additional care at home. A new carer arrived, excited to meet her new client and full of warmth and kindness. Her name was Sabira, and before long she confided to my dad that she had four young sons, who were eagerly awaiting news of her meeting with him. Listening from the next room, I wondered if this might be a slightly over-the-top approach to winning over new clientele. As I continued to eavesdrop, it now appeared that Sabira would like a selfie with my dad to show to her sons. It seemed that she had read his notes only to discover that, for over fifty years, dad had been a samurai warrior. Initially I was incredulous at what could well be the best kept secret our family has sat on over the years, when slowly the dawn of realisation began to break.

Dad was one of the longest serving Samaritan volunteers in the UK, volunteering for over fifty years. Many minutes of laughter ensued between the three of us as my dad and I gently corrected Sabira of her genuine mistake. Since that day we have encouraged Dad that this may be something he should work to his advantage, ensuring that he receives the best home care in the neighbourhood. The humorous image of a possible costume opportunity, with sword strategically placed and an appropriately warrior-like pose, was not lost on this quiet and beautifully gentle man.

At the start of this book I want to examine afresh the father heart of God. Is He Samaritan or samurai?

Have we got caught up in a similar kind of cosmic mistaken identity? In many ways our approach to God as Father will be inevitably linked to our experience of earthly fathering. Speaking from my own experience, and without wanting to gloat, I am sincerely grateful that my understanding and deep awareness of being unconditionally loved by God as Father has been etched on my heart from a very early age.

> 'The LORD is gracious and compassionate, slow to anger and rich in love.' Psalm 145:8

My earthly father's love for me has always served as a beautiful demonstration of what our heavenly Father's love is like. My dad is a man who has delighted in my successes, picked me up after my failures and cheered me on throughout the race of my life. He is to this day a remarkable man of warmth, grace and deep, quiet love.

If, in contrast, we have known absent or dysfunctional fathering here on earth, God may well seem a distant, punitive figure who we never allow to come close, who we never fully trust. One of the lies that take root as a consequence of this, is that we are not lovable – which can lead us into an addiction to looking for that love and approval in unhelpful places. Why did He let our earthly fathers wound and abandon us so much? I believe God is with us on the journey of restoration and mending. It is a tough road as we unlearn some of the false messages we have heard and believed. We will need the Bible, His Word spoken to us, to start to replace the lies with the truth of God's universal, unconditional love. As it says in the psalms, 'The LORD is gracious and compassionate, slow to anger and rich in love' (Psa. 145:8).

At the very core of each of us is a desire to give and receive love, in a way that reflects God's nature. In His deep, rescuing love we have a Father who is *for* us no matter what; we have an advocate for life. We have the one who holds the whole of eternity in His hands, cheering us on throughout every broken and beautiful day of our lives. He is *the* Samaritan, counsellor, our ever-present help in times of trouble – but He is also our samurai, the one who fights for us, who even fought death for us and won.

God, as our heavenly Father, is judge and jury over our lives but not only is He full of truth, He is full of grace. The loving grace that loves us too much to let us go on sinning and hurting ourselves and others. The Father, who constantly picks us up and heals our wounds; the Father, who has given us stories, gifts, and life, has also given us rules for our freedom. If in life we have had the graceful side of God's fatherhood wonderfully modelled, we are richly blessed and profoundly grateful. Yet herein lies a personal challenge. There is a danger that we can then start to take this grace so much for granted that we lose the awe and wonder of the judgment of the samurai. God has become too much the Samaritan – to the point that the sense of judgment and the enmity we naturally deserve can be swallowed up in our own personal absolution.

So how can we understand and know God as both samurai and Samaritan; warrior and helper? The answer is through Jesus Christ, who was and is God and who is full of grace and truth. He came and lived among us as a human being, to show us what God is really like and to demonstrate His unconditional love for us. As it is expressed in John, 'We have seen his glory, the glory of the one and only Son, who came from the Father, full of grace and truth' (John 1:14).

So whether we relate to God the Father more as Samaritan or samurai, we can allow the whole of His fatherhood, the whole of His love, to reveal both grace and truth in our lives, and to lovingly direct His Spirit where we need His reconstruction and restoration the most.

'If we ask God why He allows evil and suffering and come to look at the cross of Jesus, we still don't know what the answer is. But we do now know what the answer is not... it cannot be that He doesn't love us.' Timothy Keller[1]

God is the Father who loves us with an everlasting love and who, in the sacrificial death of His Son Jesus, shows He thinks that we are worth dying for. He is Samaritan *and* samurai and loves us too much to let us stay as we are. Like the dog who thinks his name is No, we will need help adjusting our hearing to begin to hear the whisper of His beautiful 'yes' spoken to us! Let's refuse to listen to the 'no' we might have heard telling us that 'we are not lovable' and choose to tune into the 'yes' of the fact that we are loved unconditionally.

TWO

LAUGHTER –
A MOTHER'S
GIFT

For my mum's funeral, I had written a eulogy that I knew I would find difficult to read on the day. So I asked the minister conducting the service to read it for me. Having what I would like to describe as artistically aesthetic handwriting, I am somewhat prone to illegibility. The lovely minister began to read my eulogy and we listened as he reminded us of her wonderful sense of humour and her impeccable comic timing. 'Her life,' he said, 'was an incredible reminder to laugh every day, to live freely and lightly, to find humour where others couldn't see it.'

Moving on, he spoke of mum's generosity of heart and of her great love for preserves, both giving and receiving them. Our grieving pew were stopped midway through our tears of remembrance. Who knew mum had a secret jam obsession? Which of us, hand on heart, could declare this generosity with preserves as one of the most memorable things about our mum's 73 years on earth? In a hilarious misreading of my carefully worded, if illegible, script, 'presents' had been read as 'preserves'. We held our peace as a family and to this day I'm sure many people's act of kindness towards my dad may well have come in the form of the odd jar of handmade preserve. 'How he must be missing Mavis and her jam!'

While not, perhaps, a particularly profound story, it meant so much to us to laugh on a day when we were celebrating the life of a woman who loved to laugh, and who brought that gift with her into some of the most challenging situations in her life. In life and, it seems, in death, she was teaching us the power of laughter as a bridge between people and as a bringer of light relief in the darkest of places. Laughter to me is one of God's most wise and wonderful gifts and I'm sure my mum would agree.

'The saint knows
That the spiritual path
Is a sublime chess game with God

And that the Beloved
Has just made a Fantastic Move

That the saint is now continually
Tripping over Joy
And bursting out in Laughter
And saying, "I Surrender!"

Whereas, my dear,
I am afraid you still think
You have a thousand serious moves.' Hafiz[2]

Laughter is part of our shared global language and Jesus knew it was one of the best ways of letting His message be understood. He often states the obvious, in order to make the disciples and the crowds listen, for example in this verse from Mark: 'It is not the healthy who need a doctor, but those who are ill. I have not come to call the righteous, but sinners' (Mark 2:17).

Jesus is also a master of the visual comic image,

painting pictures with His words that would have really entertained as well as being memorable and accessible to all. In Luke, He uses common animals to make His point about being too zealous regarding the Sabbath. 'If one of you has a child or an ox that falls into a well on the Sabbath day, will you not immediately pull it out?' (Luke 14:5). Whether it's oxen in wells or a camel through the eye of a needle (Matt. 19:24), Jesus uses imagery to enable the crowd of listeners to recognise aspects of themselves and to apply common sense. Jesus wanted His followers to be free from living under the unyielding oppression of the law, and to live instead in the beautiful freedom of the kingdom He is to introduce – one where humour plays a brilliant part.

Of course, the parables that Jesus told are well-known and well-remembered for their use of imagery. When He originally told them, He would have had His listeners transfixed with the observational humour they so cleverly contained. Jesus would sketch out a comedy with characters, and I can almost imagine Him putting on a voice or an accent as He spoke. The one in particular that I can almost hear Him performing is the story of the Pharisee and the tax collector (Luke 18:9–14). Jesus sets the scene: two men went up to the temple to pray, one a Pharisee, the other a tax collector. The Pharisee prays: 'God, I thank you that I am not like other people – robbers,

evildoers, adulterers – or even like this tax collector.'
In sharp and brilliant contrast the tax collector cries
out, 'God, have mercy on me, a sinner.' This is a totally
deliberate comic attempt to reverse the role of 'the
good guy'. Everyone will have expected the Pharisee
to come out of this as the prayer expert. Using humour
and shock tactics we see the traditional villain, the
tax collector, come out of this well, while the 'hero'
Pharisee is mocked with gentle derision by Jesus'
comic parody. Jesus shows that God is interested in the
sincere heartfelt prayer of the sinner, not in a polished
prayer performance.

As a performer who loves comedy myself, I know
the value of laughter as a tool to both entertain and
to teach. It is a wonderful feeling when the audience
laughs with you, acknowledging in a self-deprecating
manner, that we know how something feels. Jesus, it
seems, was a master at this. He used humour to expose
what lies within us all so that, with laughter, we can
admit that, 'I do that, I feel like that, I pray like that...'

In the Old Testament we also find the value of humour
and laughter expressed. The name 'Isaac' is given to the
son of Abraham and Sarah. His name means 'he laughs'
or 'laughter'. When Isaac is born to Sarah, she declares,
'God has brought me laughter, and everyone who hears
about this will laugh with me' (Gen. 21:6). Sarah sees
that laughter will bring people together. Laughter is part
of worship. Laughter speaks to me of abundant life – it

speaks of a God who is loving, generous and who loves to see our joy in the world He has made.

'If love is the treasure, laughter is the key'
Yakov Smirnoff

The dog who thinks his name is No sees the whole world as a negative. He hears and sees 'no'. For most of my teenage years I saw the Christian faith as a series of 'no's. The Bible was a rule book setting out a precarious moral tightrope that I knew I would continually fall off. Discovering the verse in John's Gospel where Jesus says, 'I have come in order that you might have life – life in all its fullness' (John 10:10, GNT) was a personal revelation. I discovered, if you like, that my name was not No, that the legalism of the moral tightrope was not the way of Jesus Christ. Maybe for you the lie or 'no' you have believed is that all faith will do is stop you from enjoying this amazing gift that is life; that faith and fun don't mix. The truth, or 'yes', is in fact that humour is a gift from a generous God. He wants fullness for your life, laughter for your heart, joy for your journey. Yes – He has given us a law, but it is a law that protects us, a law that keeps us close to God and His abundant life, now and in eternity.

THREE

MISTAKES – I'VE MADE A FEW!

In my first year as a newly-qualified teacher I had a very funny reminder of the advantages of failure. I was setting up my Year Seven (11-year-olds) drama class with great enthusiasm (on my part at least). I had been teaching them for several weeks and was, or so I thought, beginning to build a relationship with them. On this particular day, my lesson was being appraised and so, of course, I was silently praying that all would go extremely well.

'You are the chosen class,' I declared, 'you are the guinea pigs in a wonderful experiment. Imagine a millionaire has given us one million pounds to go on a surprise trip to an unknown destination. All we have to do is pack a bag each and together turn up at the airport. So imagine it's the night before we are due to go. In pairs, you are going to begin to role play this; the planning, the excitement. We don't know what language is spoken, how to pack for an unknown climate or what currency we will need. You are the guinea pigs in this, remember, and if you make this work, we will really have a great adventure. So, in pairs, it's the night before, off you go.'

And so I released them into their pairs with a final dramatic flourish. Looking bewildered and muttering slightly under their breath, off they went to undertake the acting exercise, while being observed by my supervisor. It wasn't long before some really strange behaviour started to spread across the room – high pitched squeaking, children running around (mostly on all fours) some twitching of noses and very little in the way of the animated role play of sensible students planning for an imagined, once-in-a-lifetime trip. Embarrassed and humiliated in front of my (annoyingly somewhat amused) tutor, I called the class back together.

'I thought you were better than this, Year Seven,' I declared in my most severe tone. 'Very few of you are on task, no one appears to be taking this seriously in front of our visitor and if I'm honest I'm incredibly disappointed in you.' Instead of any kind of defiance, rows of crestfallen faces stared back at me, hurt and dejected. Finally a lovely, conscientious girl called Naomi raised a tremulous hand, 'We are trying so hard Miss Moore, but we don't even know how guinea pigs speak, let alone what they take on holiday.'

This lovely group had been trying very hard to undertake the somewhat dubious challenge set by their teacher, in front of a visitor, of being guinea pigs, packing in preparation for a surprise once-in-a-lifetime trip anywhere in world. As I replayed the images of the last ten minutes in my mind, of twitching noses and jerky hand gestures with hands rolled into paw-like fists, enlightenment came. My supervisor had been ahead of me and had witnessed the whole comedic scene. Through almost uncontrollable laughter, that he and I were sharing, I addressed the bewildered group.

'I am so sorry, Year Seven. This is completely my fault. There is an expression called "being a guinea pig in an experiment", that you obviously haven't heard and, quite understandably, have taken it literally. I should have learnt by now that it is up to me, as your teacher, to give you clear instructions. I'm so sorry I shouted at you all, especially as you had been trying so hard to do such a strange piece of theatre. Will you forgive me?'

'Of course,' they chorused as one (well that's how I remember it!), laughing too, although probably still not quite sure why. Speaking afterwards to my supervisor, a wonderfully wise and gentle man, he said something I have never forgotten. 'That was wonderful,' he commented, without a hint of sarcasm. Had he, I wondered to myself, just witnessed a completely different lesson to the one in which I had failed so badly? 'Do you know, Judy, you may well be the only adult who has ever asked for their forgiveness, who has publically put right a wrong, an injustice? I suspect they will trust you even more now and will work even harder to learn from you because of your openness and vulnerability.' He was to be proved right, and my relationship with that class throughout the five years of teaching them, remained one of my favourites.

'Success is not final, failure is not fatal: it is the courage to continue that counts.' Unknown

They say that, in the UK at least, our greatest fear is still public speaking. I'm not sure if that is true but it certainly underlines how fearful we are of failing, and how doing so publically, is abhorrent to so many of us. In my life, I have experienced failure. I have lived through a very public relationship break-up, with many people calling no doubt from the wings, 'we told you so!' I resisted the call to church leadership for almost a year, trying to frame my disobedience at the time in a whole host of ways. In short, I know what it is to fail. But equally, I know a God who redeems our failure, who takes our falling down as a chance to draw even closer, and even to stoop down, to pick us up.

'My grace is sufficient for you, for my power is made perfect in weakness. Therefore I will boast even more gladly about my weaknesses, so that Christ's power may rest on me.' 2 Corinthians 12:9

I'm not quite sure when my speaking ministry began, but I do remember someone who helped me to start.

A man called John used to join the family holidays we ran each year when I was acting with the Saltmine Theatre Company. He and his wife Alison had been in Devon and had bought me a present that, even to this day, serves as a reminder of my frailty. It was a beautiful glass tealight holder covered with handmade paper. When the candle inside was lit, it was clear that where the light shone at its brightest, was where the surrounding paper was at its most fragile. John spoke about the kind of leader I would become (prophetically, as it turned out), reassuring me that God wanted to use my vulnerability and my flaws to show His power and His strength. As the Bible says, 'My grace is sufficient for you, for my power is made perfect in weakness. Therefore I will boast even more gladly about my weaknesses, so that Christ's power may rest on me' (2 Cor. 12:9).

Increasingly, as a nation we are longing for authenticity, as we recognise our own fears and failures and look for those who will join us in saying that we are broken. The gospel and ministry of Jesus is counter-cultural in this area. The Bible has often been heralded as a book of heroic failures, such as David, Jonah and Peter. God will use our failures every bit as much as our successes. The gospel of Jesus Christ is one that embraces all our failures and brokenness, and redeems us and turns our life around. Failure can be one of our greatest teachers. Grace is so hard for us to grasp. Sometimes it is failure that helps us to fall into grace in a way we may not have discovered had we only ever known success. Perhaps the very thing we have feared – failure in life – was an opportunity for grace to rescue us. The lie (or 'no') that your failures define you in a negative way is replaced with the truth (or 'yes') that the experience of failing can be the making and shaping of you in a positive way.

FOUR

A POWERFUL WEAPON

Teaching poetry to 12-year-olds on a very warm Friday afternoon can be challenging. The week before, the class had studied the poem, *What has happened to Lulu?* I had set the students the task of imagining that they were Lulu, who has run away from home. They were to write dialogue that may have preceded Lulu's sudden departure.

One particular boy (who I will refer to as 'J') stood to read his script aloud. 'J' had used his imagination a little too freely and Lulu had become a drug-taking, bisexual prostitute who was running away to experience explicit sexual freedom. My teacher's instinct was that 'J', rather than testing his imaginative powers, was more interested in seeing if he could embarrass his young, newly-qualified, female teacher. My response was to turn the tables on him in front of his classmates. 'If, for one moment, you wrote this script to embarrass me, I think the only person who is embarrassed now, is you,' was my parting shot, as he returned, red-faced to his seat. (I was still learning and would later temper my approach – well, very slightly!)

I don't know if he had spent the whole week planning his revenge, but as we began the English lesson, 'J' had definitely come prepared. We were reading poetry aloud when, from the back of the room, he jumped to his feet brandishing a gun. Everything went into slow motion. I couldn't think. I thought my legs would give way under me. It is truly amazing, however, what the responsibility for 30 young 12-year-olds will do to focus the mind. Inwardly, I spoke the name of Jesus over and over again. Outwardly, I calmly asked 'J' to put the gun down as someone could get hurt. He aimed it at me and said with a mocking voice, 'You're going to make me, are you Miss?' 'No,' I replied, 'you're much stronger than me, but please put it down.' I continued to repeat the name of Jesus in my head while not moving at all, rooted to the spot. I asked again if he would put the gun down.

What happened next still fills me with amazement. As if a tranquilliser dart had gone into his body, my young would-be assassin did just as I asked. He put the gun under his chair and sat down. I'm not sure if this was post-traumatic shock or the behaviour of a new and naïve teacher, but I then carried on with the lesson. I suppose I should have done something to remove 'J' and his gun from the other children, but instead we carried on dutifully reading poetry until the lesson ended. As soon as the bell rang, I sent for a duty deputy and 'J' was led away. Later, the gun was revealed to be an air gun that 'J' was supposedly 'looking after' for his aunt.

Although initially suspended from school, 'J' did return and I agreed to continue to teach him. We even ended up having a good teacher–student relationship, with some light-hearted exchanges about leaving weapons at the door during poetry lessons. Although this episode gave me, as a new teacher, a reputation of having hard-core courage, I honestly don't remember ever being so scared!

> 'The light shines in the darkness, and the darkness has not overcome it.' John 1:5

I truly believe that there is incredible power in the name of Jesus. Saying His name repeatedly in my mind enabled me to remain calm – despite my inner desperation. Jesus was active and working in that classroom. What Class 8C witnessed that day was the miraculous power of the name of Jesus. I cried out to Him and He answered me. The Bible tells us that, 'The light shines in the darkness, and the darkness has not overcome it' (John 1:5). The darkness hasn't even understood the light. Darkness is a defeated enemy. When Stoke-on-Trent, Staffordshire was voted one of the worst places to live in the UK in 2007, the churches there got together and said, 'If our city is one of darkness, it is not about the power of that darkness; it is about us coming together in prayer and unity to show the true quality of the light.'

In another chapter, I'll refer to the story of the ten Boom family and our adaptation of *The Hiding Place* for the stage. In the story, when one of the guards raiding the family's little clock shop tries to hit Corrie with his gun, she shouts the name of Jesus and the guard's arm freezes midair. The very name of Jesus offends and disempowers him so much that the guard asks Corrie never to speak it again.

In the Bible, we see many instances demonstrating the power within the name of Jesus. In Acts, the apostles carry on the work that they saw Jesus do, by doing it in His name; praying in the name of Jesus and believing in the power it holds to heal, to free and to deliver. We read in Philippians 'that at the name of Jesus every knee should bow, in heaven and on earth and under the earth' (Phil. 2:10). We may believe the lie or 'no' that we have no power beyond ourselves, but the truth is that 'yes', there is power in the name of Jesus and it is ours to use, if we believe in Him.

FIVE

Pity-party DIVA

I have spent a great deal of my life touring in a whole variety of theatre productions. Touring, as many of you will know, is both a wonderful privilege and at times, extremely tough. This story begins not long after my mum had died, which had been very sudden. Like many of us, I was escaping back into a world that I thought would comfort me with its familiarity, only to find it taunting me with that very familiarity when no one else's world seemed to have changed.

W.H. Auden's poem *Funeral Blues*[3] includes a line that I find particularly insightful: 'Stop all the clocks, cut off the telephone, Prevent the dog from barking with a juicy bone'. Grief can so easily isolate us from the world we once knew.

We were performing the play *The Cross and The Switchblade*. The venue felt soulless with poor sports-hall-like acoustics. The show had gone down very well but I was not at all pleased with my own performance. I was playing the incredibly saintly Gwen Wilkerson, wife of David Wilkerson, and to be honest it felt like a bit of a stretch. I just wasn't feeling it. With more bad news from home about another friend of the family being seriously unwell, I started to spiral down into a bit of an epic pity-party. I didn't want to be on the road. I didn't want to be playing someone saintly. I wanted to play someone sassy and edgy and, yes, angry! Feeling desperate and incredibly low, I prayed my very best consumerist prayer: 'Please God, can my host tonight live in a beautiful house and take care of me? Please can I have an en-suite bathroom, a glass of wine and candles round the bath?' I confessed my deeply mature prayer to several of my fellow actors who awaited my host's arrival with interest.

Shortly after, a motorbike pulled up noisily outside the venue, dropped off a woman and sped off into the night. This woman, whom we shall call Pat, had a shaved head, tattoos, and strode into the venue with purpose. Convinced that she was not for me – especially as she now had no transport – I wondered who she might have come for. Imagine my amazement as Pat called out my name. 'Judy? Is there someone here called Judy? She's staying with me tonight.' My initial thought was, *God hates me. Whatever I ask of Him, He literally does the opposite.* 'Here I am,' I smiled weakly.

We got into the hire-car that had been organised (an automatic), which I drove (it being only my second time ever driving an automatic car) to her home. Pat's flat was small; I was sleeping where her children would normally have slept. I was grumpy, silent, and unfriendly. Sitting on the small bed, I texted my then boyfriend: 'I can't do this.'

Pat had offered me tea, so I went down resolving to get myself some manners. As I joined my host, she seemed quiet and nervous. Pat then apologised, explaining that she had never hosted a Christian before and admitted that she was quite anxious. 'Was everything alright for you?' she asked. Feeling immediately humbled by her kindness and increasingly ashamed of my attitude, we had some tea and began to share stories. Before long it began to unfold that Pat was very new to Christianity, having been a witch for most of her adult life. A few years ago, she had stabbed her abusive husband in self-defence. At this point, and to my shame, I silently questioned to myself whether I was part of some sort of trick, a kind of staged wind-up worthy of Ant and Dec or (for older readers) Jeremy Beadle! Any minute now the camera crew would be revealed, the producer would laughingly reveal my tormentors and all would be well again.

Pat was a good mum, and some Christian women, who she saw every day on the school run, had prayed for her over the years to come to know Jesus. At the time of the aforementioned incident with her husband, Pat had feared she would lose custody of her children. Not realising that these women were praying for her so fervently, she found herself, on this desperate day, drawn towards one of their homes. In deep distress, Pat described almost falling into one woman's arms and telling her she was lost. This Christian lady called her husband, and together they prayed for Pat to come to know Jesus, the only one they knew who could rescue her life. Having come to faith and believing in the power of Jesus with all her heart, Pat still found it hard to attend a church, feeling as though she did not belong in that culture. She missed her old friends from her witchcraft days and decided to go back one last time to her Satanist meeting.

She was late, Pat said, and walked in at the back. As she moved forward into the body of the people meeting, the man leading the service suddenly cowered and shrank back. 'Get out of here!' he shouted, 'There is a power in you that is too much for us. Get out!' As a Christian of just a few weeks, the power that was within Pat was greater than any work of the enemy!

Needless to say, with goosebumps on my skin and tears pouring down my face, realisation came. This wonderfully brave woman, in sharing her story with me, had done what no scented candles or en-suite bathroom could ever have done. She had reminded me of the resurrection power of Jesus that lives in each of us. In my desperate state, He had lifted my perspective to who He was and what He was able to do.

> 'he who is in you is greater than he who is in the world.' 1 John 4:4 (ESVUK)

This has always been one of my favourite stories from my life on the road – not because I come out of it particularly well, but because God does. We see Him manoeuvring events and crafting situations so that I am exactly where I'm meant to be, to hear exactly what I need to hear, which is that, 'he who is in you is greater than he who is in the world' (1 John 4:4, ESVUK).

We need to remember that because of Jesus' death and resurrection, the devil is defeated. Jesus said, 'It is finished' (John 19:30). We fight *from* a position of victory, not *for* a position of victory. Perhaps for many of us, we have bought into the idea of a level cosmic playing field, a literal tug of war as portrayed in both classic Greek and some contemporary theatre. The devil on one side, God on the other, with poor humanity torn between the two. Scripture tells us that this is far from true. Jesus says, 'take heart! I have overcome the world' (John 16:33). The devil is under our feet and is defeated for all time. God is above all powers, all kingdoms, all created things – including evil.

We are warned in Scripture not to be ignorant of the devil's schemes and this is undoubtedly true, with evil so prevalent in our world today. But I do sometimes think we give him a little too much credit. 'The devil made me do it' is sometimes a way to absolve ourselves of our own responsibility to make wise choices. Common sense is spiritual too!

C.S. Lewis addresses this brilliantly in his book *The Screwtape Letters*[4]: 'It is funny how mortals always picture us putting things into their minds: in reality our best work is done by keeping things out.' In short, the more of God's truth we can hide in our heart, the more we allow the fruits of His Holy Spirit to renew our minds – we will start to recognise the tone of the enemy's voice and to reject the lies and falsehoods of his schemes.

'It is funny how mortals always picture us putting things into their minds: in reality our best work is done by keeping things out'.
C.S. Lewis, *The Screwtape Letters*[4]

John Nash, in the biography of his life *A Beautiful Mind*[5], learns to train his mind towards thoughts that lead to life rather than death. As he struggles with the chronic condition of schizophrenia, he is slowly learning to distinguish between the tone that builds him up and the one that brings him down. His struggle reminds me of the wonderful biblical principle of thought-catching: 'We demolish arguments and every pretension that sets itself up against the knowledge of God, and we take captive every thought to make it obedient to Christ' (2 Cor. 10:5).

So at the close of this chapter, we are reminded that sometimes, the 'no' of God is for a far greater 'yes'. The 'no' of the crucifixion was met with the glorious 'yes' of the resurrection. The dog who thought his name was No had perhaps only heard half a story. On my diva pity-party day when I thought God was literally saying 'no' to everything, His 'yes' was immeasurably more beautiful than I could ever have hoped – a reminder of His resurrection power!

SIX

DIVINE DNA

We were spending the day in Brinsford Prison for young offenders. As a touring theatre company, we had a variety of venues, no two shows were ever the same and no two audience responses were identical. Sometimes we would do a full-length play in prison, for example, *Keep taking the tablets*, a soap opera about the Ten Commandments (see what we did there!) and sometimes we would weave together a variety of sketches around a theme. At the end of a show of the latter style of performance, I was sharing with the inmates a memory from my primary school days: my incredible joy when, having placed my finger into paint and then onto paper again, I discovered for the first time that my finger print was unique. No matter whether I had a brother, a sister or an identical twin, no one shared the same print as me. At which point the heckling began. 'That's why we're here... why would you say that? We hate the fact that we're here because of DNA!' DNA, it turns out, is not a subject for joy and childlike delight in a prison context. A valuable lesson for a naïve actress.

Fast forward a few years; same prison, different crowd. We were in the chapel, reading from the Psalms with a group of young offenders we had been talking to all week. We reached the part where the psalmist says, 'you created my inmost being; you knit me together in my mother's womb... all the days ordained for me were written in your book' (Psa. 139:13,16).

'This is lies, Miss!' said one of the men. 'I'm not listening to any more of this!' (I may have omitted some colourful language here!) The young prisoner went on to tell me how he had known from the age of five that he was a mistake; how neither of his parents planned or wanted him. 'I'm a mistake,' he declared defiantly, 'I'm a mistake, so there is no plan and I do what I like.'

We went on to share with him that God has a plan for every life and that He really wanted this young man to be born. I also shared with him how his humour had helped me not feel my usual nerves about going into the prison; how we had all commented on his kindness in feeding digestive biscuits to his pet pigeon through the bars of his cell window and how, even in that week, he had made a positive impact on us. He looked at us, listening in disbelief and I noticed tears in his eyes which he quickly brushed away. Before we went away at the end of the day, he quietly approached me and asked if I could give him 'a copy of that poem you read – the one about God planning me and thinking me up. I'll put it on my wall to keep me out of trouble!'

'For we are God's masterpiece. He has created us anew in Christ Jesus, so we can do the good things he planned for us long ago.' Ephesians 2:10 (NLT)

I believe it tells us so much about God as our Father, and as our creator, that we are designed with our own plan and purpose. In Ephesians, Paul writes, 'For we are God's masterpiece. He has created us anew in Christ Jesus, so we can do the good things he planned for us long ago' (Eph. 2:10, NLT). This verse speaks to me of the opportunity for every person to have an impact, to touch this world in a way that fits with their particular personality and talent. For many years now, I have worked with various personality profiling tests. These are such fantastic tools that unlock the potential residing inside every one of us, to be the very best that we can be. The premise is that these tests reveal key personality traits, the talents and ways of being that we just can't help but live out. For example, we don't aim to be 'empathetic' or 'strategic' – we just naturally are.

DNA may be a giveaway for the criminal, but our divine DNA is an incredible indicator of the role and purpose for every life with its unique potential. The 'no' – that we are a mistake – is a lie, the truth or the 'yes' is that God thought you up and planned for you to be born.

SEVEN

The camel KNOWS the WAY

One of my great life adventures was a ten-day trek across the Sinai Peninsula to raise money for the work of the Saltmine Theatre Company. We would walk across the desert in the day and sleep out under the stars at night (or rather, under a canvas, as it was extremely cold). The beautiful sight of the Milky Way lighting up a crisp and clear night sky is one that remains with me to this day. On the final day of our trek, our guides were to pick us up in the middle of the night to begin the ascent of Mount Sinai. We would then share Communion together at the top of the mountain, as the sun came up.

Waiting for the camels that were to take us up the mountain, I suddenly found myself whisked away, not in a romantic sense, but physically whisked away without warning. 'You will go on my camel please,' said a guide, and with this declaration I was unceremoniously lifted on to a camel. Without any introductions to the man, or indeed the camel, we were off into the darkness. After a while I could just make out, in the pitch dark, that we were following a path up the side of the mountain. The path was incredibly close to the edge. I was equally aware that none of my fellow trekkers were anywhere to be seen. A growing sense of panic started to rise in me. Who was this man? I seemed to be literally trusting him with my life!

The camel moved along the path up the mountain, getting closer and closer to the edge. All the time I was silently praying and wondering if I would ever see any of my loved ones again. I clung on for dear life as we continued to career up the precipice. Although finding it increasingly hard to, I looked down and saw a string of lights looking like Christmas fairy lights twinkling on the path below. It was my fellow travellers, slowly making their way up the same path, seemingly linked together. Considerably reassured by this sight, I looked back to my camel and my now smiling companion and slowly something occurred to me. The camel knew every step of this mountain. He had walked this way so many times before that he didn't even hesitate, just felt his way in the darkness on every precarious part of the path. What appeared to me to be a step into the unknown was, for him, part of a journey he did every day. Well, of course we made it to the top of the mountain and, gratefully reunited with my fellow travellers, I could relate my experience and laugh as we broke bread together and worshipped God.

To this day I'm not sure why I was picked to go ahead of the group but, if I'm honest, the episode has been a bit of a metaphor for my life!

'He will not let your foot slip – he who watches over you will not slumber' Psalm 121:3

My journey into church leadership has been one that I never really sought out, and I have been slightly disarmed by people's belief in me. I am profoundly grateful to those on the journey of leading with me who have helped to light the path, to see beyond what I could see and have led me to trust and hold onto God throughout the adventure. There has always been that sense of being an imposter, scooped up in the night and put on an unknown camel ahead of the herd. Yet leadership has rarely been as lonely as I might have imagined. I'm a passionate believer in 'team', and in leading within a team of people with different personalities.

Guidance, in my life, has been an interesting journey too. With the gift of discernment from God the Holy Spirit, I can, quite often, clearly see the track ahead for those I lead and pastor. However, I find it much more difficult to trust and discern God's way ahead for me personally. Yet when I look back over my life so far, much like looking down the mountain path and seeing the lights, I can see so clearly how He has led me and stopped me from falling. As the psalmist says, 'He will not let your foot slip – he who watches over you will not slumber' (Psa. 121:3).

Sometimes we can make the guidance of God into a sort of puzzle that we have to work at in order to discern God's elusive path for us. In the past, I have been fearful of 'getting it wrong' for God's plan A for my life – as if God wasn't big enough to have a plan B, C, or D! I am now much more convinced of the words of the hymn, 'He knows the way He taketh, and I will walk with Him'.[6] God has promised that if we walk closely with Him,

He will lead us. In the Old Testament book of Exodus, we read that God would talk with Moses clearly, not in riddles but as if talking with a friend (Exod. 33:11).

'The LORD confides in those who fear him'
Psalm 25:14

I have found the following 'Five Cs of Guidance' to be a help when seeking to hear from God. Compare what you feel you have heard with:

1. Counsel of Scripture (Does this fit with what the Bible says?)
2. Counsel of the Holy Spirit
3. Counsel of the saints (Seek the opinions of Christians you respect)
4. Common sense
5. Circumstances

Occasionally, I have gone for number three, and number five – rather than trusting the Spirit-given promptings. I have also fought to make something that I *felt* I had heard from God come about, when it ultimately hadn't been from God at all.

I recommend we start with number one and move forwards from there. The most common ways God has always spoken to His people is through the Bible and through the Holy Spirit. God knows us intimately and profoundly, and He guides and even 'confides in those who fear Him' (Psa. 25:14). He knows who we are and what is best for us. That might mean that He doesn't answer some of our prayers as we would like, even those that are said during painful times. I have learnt to thank God for seemingly unanswered prayers because His ways are higher (Isa. 55:9) and His knowledge of us is unfathomably deeper. Staying close to Him, talking to Him, reading His Word and listening to Him will help us on our journey.

A lie or 'no' that we sometimes believe is that somehow we are not good enough to hear from God. However, the truth or 'yes' is that He always hears us and delights in guiding us and lighting the path, even when it feels dark.

EIGHT

Exit
STAGE LEFT

During my theatre training, a great deal of emphasis was often placed on *making an entrance*. How the character enters the stage, clearly lets the audience know their status and the relationship they have with those who are already present. Much less attention was given, however, to the art of exiting a scene well. 'Exit, pursued by a bear' is one of theatre's best known stage directions. It appears in the third act of Shakespeare's *The Winter's Tale*, and gives the actor playing Antigonus the motivation and the emotion required for the exit. This is a rare gift for the actor!

I do not have a great track record in exiting the stage. One such exiting occasion was after a short but, I like to think memorable, appearance dressed as Obi-Wan Kenobi (of *Star Wars* fame!). I had not originally been cast in this role, you will be relieved to learn, but was a last minute stand-in for a tall male actor. It was the opening night of a tour, and gauging the width of the stage and the backstage access for the first time, the original actor realised that he could not feasibly appear in the designated costume, perform and run off stage, in time to play the piano and sing on the other side, just a minute later. With speed and first-night adrenalin, the cast agreed that I would cover for him and run on stage, virtually unnoticed, in a brief crowd scene, asking for George Lucas' autograph. I would then exit swiftly in readiness for my next costume change. Hot-footing it off stage, following my fleeting appearance, I found the exit door in the darkness. Opening it, I was suddenly immersed in broad daylight. Instead of the anticipated gentle solace of the dressing room, my wrong turn had led to a surprise appearance on the first level of a public car park, providing a rather unexpected treat for the latecomers queuing below. On this occasion I managed to swiftly retreat, with an embarrassed but stylish wave, back into the dark of the building and find my proper destination. There may be group of people who believe to this day that it was all part of a surprise welcome for the audience, but for me, it remains a truly embarrassing moment. My only comfort is that I like to think I was pretty unrecognisable in my hooded hessian cloak made for a six foot male actor.

'All the world's a stage, And all the men and women merely players; They have their exits and their entrances, And one man in his time plays many parts' William Shakespeare, *As You Like It*

A similar wrong turn on exiting the stage, brought me into the temporary captivity of a sports equipment cupboard. I was playing the role of Edna, a thoroughly disgruntled caretaker who delivers a heartfelt lesson on the correct procedure of chair stacking. After which she flounces off the stage with a final flourish of anger at the incompetence of all who fail to *stack* appropriately. My motivation was clear; I was angry, superior and enjoying my moment of power. Slamming what I believed to be the stage left exit door behind me for added effect, I turned around in horror. I appeared to be in a cupboard with no obvious handle on the inside and a large amount of sports equipment all around. With a rising sense of alarm, I realised I was trapped. I would completely miss my next cue and had no way of alerting my fellow actors to my captivity. After a few panic-stricken minutes, a fellow actor came to my aid, brilliantly weaving my release into the storyline of the play. As with all the best backstage secrets, my hope is that most of the audience were oblivious to my mistake.

One of the things I hope that both these stories highlight, is the sense of team in an acting cast and the strength of covering one another when we take a wrong turn or navigate a crisis. Over the years of working with different theatre companies and actors, we have covered each other's lines, untangled each other's microphone wires, changed each other's costumes (very little modesty backstage, I'm afraid) and improvised while waiting for late cues or entrances. Acting has sometimes been viewed as a rather egotistical and selfish profession, but my experience has been of working with selfless, generous and thoughtful performers, many of whom have become lifelong friends.

However, these backstage secrets are mainly revealed to illustrate a very real sense in life of having taken a wrong turn, become stuck or completely lost. My lack of exiting talent is partly due to an inability to see in the dark (more carrots required!), coupled with an extremely limited, maybe even non-existent, sense of direction. The invention of sat-nav and Google Maps have given me back the gift of time. Much of my life before GPS and smart phones was spent feeling irretrievably lost. Some people love a map, while I am hugely in favour of the disembodied automated voice in the car encouraging me to make a U-turn or reassuring me that I am being re-routed. I still experience a frisson of delight at times when 'Tim', my voice of choice, declares triumphantly that I have arrived at my destination!

One of the greatest lies or 'no's we can be tempted to believe is that there is no way back. Most of us, at some point, will experience that sense of searching for the exit in the dark, trapped in addictions, bad relationships or repeated mistakes. Sometimes, depression can descend with its clouds of despair and doubt. Just as few of us are immune to falling physically ill, so with mental health, we will have stronger and weaker times. Depression is not a modern day malaise, although it seems to be increasing especially among younger people. It is experienced by people in both the Old and the New Testaments of the Bible.

Elijah hopes to die and cannot see a way back from despair. He says, 'I have had enough, LORD... Take my life; I am no better than my ancestors' (1 Kings 19:4).

God's wonderful response to Elijah under the broom tree is to feed him and advise him to rest. The Bible here is giving guidance of practical application when taking care of our own mental and emotional health. Elijah is burnt out. He has been victorious but now is out of hope, out of energy and out of answers. He can't see a way out, but God can. God can always see in the dark even when we can't.

In my life, I have hit dead ends and disappointments; I didn't go to the university I wanted to go to, I didn't marry the man I thought I would. I have sat on several beaches crying, thinking my life was over and believing the lies that said I would never change, never succeed, never be happy. However, God has always shown me a way out, a way forward, a path of release and redemption. He dreams up paths that may differ from the ones you and I have planned, but which are nevertheless good, deeply fulfilling and perhaps even better.

In the New Testament, both Peter and Judas fail Jesus, but whereas Judas believes the lie that there is no way back and takes his own life, Peter comes to Jesus with his feelings of failure and shame, and is asked to be the shepherd of Christ's sheep, of His precious lambs. If you are reading this book and you believe that there is no way back from something you have done or something that may have happened to you, please allow this truth from Isaiah to speak to you: 'I will turn the darkness into light before them and make the rough places smooth' (Isa. 42:16). The prophet Isaiah is using these words on behalf of God, who rescued the Israelites from captivity in Egypt, who set prisoners free from wrongful imprisonment and who, believe it or not, has a rescue plan for you too.

> 'I will turn the darkness into light before them and make the rough places smooth.' Isaiah 42:16

Nicky Cruz was a notorious New York gang leader and murderer. God sent a Presbyterian minister called David Wilkerson from Pennsylvania to show him there was a way out for him and his gang. David daily pursued Nicky on the streets of New York, telling him he would one day grow tired of running from the unrelenting, unstoppable love of Jesus Christ. One such day came and Nicky found himself rescued, loved and ultimately restored.

There is a way out, a Plan B, a re-routing of the direction your life may be taking. Sometimes it takes another person to help you find it, as with my grateful release from the equipment cupboard. So often there can be someone who is there to help in our time of darkness. For Nicky Cruz it was David Wilkerson, for me it was my sister who prayed for me and somehow got me to agree to go to a beach mission. If you are having a tough time with suicidal or despairing thoughts, I pray that God will lead you to the right person who will in turn guide you to Jesus Christ, the one who has made a way out of the darkness and a path to life and hope through His love.

'O God of such truth as sweeps away all lies, of such grace as shrivels all excuses, come now to find us, for we have lost ourselves in a shuffle of disguises and the rattle of empty words.
Let your Spirit move mercifully to recreate us from the chaos of our lives.
We have been careless of our days, our loves, our gifts, our chances...
Our prayer is to change, O God, not out of despair of self but for love of you,
and for the selves we long to become before we simply waste away.
Let your mercy move in and through us now...
Amen.' Ted Loder, *My Heart in My Mouth*[7]

NINE

THE JOY OF GIVING

Bulgaria is a beautiful country, in areas broken and barren yet constantly being rebuilt. As part of working for the charity the Saltmine Trust, I have been privileged to visit amazing places, sample diverse cultures and meet wonderful people. One such person was a very young boy who taught me an incredible biblical truth and life lesson. He was a small Bulgarian child living in an orphanage called Dragadanavo. Visiting Dragadanavo was like arriving at a place where human compassion had not fully infiltrated. A child could be sent to live in an orphanage for minor crimes such as stealing potatoes to feed family members.

To be honest, I was apprehensive of this visit and as we drove up to the entrance, the building confirmed all my worst fears. The façade of the building was grey and foreboding, resembling a prison camp from the Second World War. The outside created a gloomy air of disproportionate punishments and draconian measures that might be carried out within. Then, as we approached closer, a tidal wave of colour cascaded from its doors. Dressed in ill-fitting clothes of every conceivable colour, children streamed towards us. Full of warmth and eagerness – their welcome was the antithesis of anything I had expected. In this dreary place was life, vitality and irrepressible hope in abundance. An eight-year-old girl, who had dared to steal apples to feed her younger siblings, took my hand and led me inside.

The Saltmine Trust had sent bedspreads for every child in the orphanage, lovingly handmade by charity supporters. Another little boy, guiding me towards his bed in the communal sleeping area, proudly indicated the cover we had sent. As I admired the cover and looked around the room, I noticed that next to every bed, there was a table displaying toys or possessions that each child treasured. This little boy's table was sparse, with just one small calendar prominently displayed, whereas other children had several belongings. *Everyone else has more than he does,* I thought, as I admired the little calendar with animals depicted on each month and, what looked like, accompanying Bible verses in Bulgarian. This particular month had a picture of a fox. I stroked the face of the fox tenderly wanting to make up for the fact that, apart from his clothes and the bedspread, this was all he owned in the world. Whether or not he thought I had a deep liking for foxes, the boy looked pleased at my response to his calendar and gave me a beautiful smile.

'When we give cheerfully and accept gratefully everyone is blessed' Maya Angelou

All too soon, our day with the children came to an end and my little smiling companion, still holding my hand, accompanied me to meet the rest of our party.

As the coach drew round to the front of the building and we began to take our leave, my small friend tugged at my skirt. He was clearly very excited and was hiding something behind his back. With a little flourish, he presented me with a gift, his calendar, his only possession! My immediate reaction was to protest and I tried to give it back. 'Thank you so much but, of course, you must keep it,' I began, but he persisted, with his arms outstretched. In that moment he became one of my life's teachers. Here was a boy whose spirit was light and free who, despite his horrible surroundings, continued to display generosity. He intuitively knew what Jesus meant when Jesus said, 'It is more blessed to give than to receive' (Acts 20:35). I took his present and kept it as a tangible reminder of the joy of giving and the beauty of a generous heart.

'It is more blessed to give than to receive' Acts 20:35

In the Bible we read of the widow who gave two copper coins into the temple treasury (Mark 12:41–43). Jesus, observing her as well as the many rich people giving much more, points out to His disciples that the rich 'gave out of their wealth; but she, out of her poverty, put in everything – all she had to live on' (v44).

> 'Give, but give until it hurts' Mother Teresa

Regularly we are given to believe that what we acquire and gain in life brings us happiness and identity. My little Bulgarian teacher however, who had very little, wanted to give me what he had and seemed very happy to do so. Compared to other countries, most people in the UK are reasonably wealthy, but as a nation, current mental health surveys suggest that we are unhappier than we were during the war years. We still have so many lessons to learn to stay generous and to grow in the art of giving. It's been said that those lucky enough to be in the wealthiest 1% of humanity owe it to the rest of humanity to think about the other 99%.

God is not a God of meanness – He is the God who has poured out His kindness and can use you, your life and your resources to make a difference, however large or small, in His world. We are most like God when we are giving. We all have something to give; the lie or 'no' is that we don't. Discover the truth or the 'yes' by finding a way to be generous even when your hands seem empty of gifts. In the words of the incredible Anne Frank: 'No one has ever become poor by giving'.[8]

TEN

No one
can imprison
your Soul

I am often asked what has been my favourite acting role. For some actors this is like having to choose between your children! In choosing, you may both flatter and offend. There is one role, however, that I feel enormously privileged to have played and that is of Corrie ten Boom. I only hope that, should we meet one day in heaven, she approved of my performance! A heroine of mine, Corrie was a watchmaker in Haarlem in the Netherlands during the Second World War. She is remembered as much for her flaws and humanity as she is for her Christian faith and courage. Along with her incredible family, she hid Jews in her home and risked her life on numerous occasions in order to protect and provide for them

Eventually, in February 1944, she was incarcerated along with her sister Betsie and witnessed the very worst of humanity. She learned of her father's death while he was in Ravensbrück prison in Germany. He was left to die on a trolley in a prison corridor. She found herself hating the Germans and she ranted at God for His lack of compassion, yet still ran Bible studies with her sister in the prison cells. She knew that the light shines in the darkness, yet at times the darkness closed in on her and she couldn't always see. There have been times in my life when I have also cried, 'Where is the light, where is the hope and victory?'

As a performer, you have licence to lament like never before, shouting in the darkness, voicing despair and releasing all your pent-up frustrations about life's suffering. In her book *The Hiding Place*[9], Corrie relates how she was interviewed by Lieutenant Rahms while in prison. She tells him that she has learned that some things are too heavy for us to carry, we cannot bear it, but our heavenly Father will carry them until we are able to. He comments on how free Corrie seems by saying, 'No one can imprison *your* soul, you are freer now than I shall ever be'. He is her captor, but says he lives in a prison far stronger than Ravensbrück. In a truly audacious way, she promises to pray for the Lieutenant, but offended and in a fit of rage, he sends her back to her cell. In a total reversal of status the scene ends, with Corrie seemingly holding all the power, not because of her situation, but because of her faith in a powerful God.

'No one can imprison *your* soul, you are freer now than I shall ever be.' Lieutenant Rahms to Corrie ten Boom while in prison.

In the final scene of our play, Corrie has been released and is preaching in Germany on forgiveness. The war is over and Corrie was set free due to an administrative error – or the miraculous intervention of God! As she reaches the end of her message, Corrie declares that 'our sins are at the bottom of the sea, washed away when we come to Christ and repent'. People are leaving the building when she is approached by a German man. He compliments her talk, but then reveals that during the war he too was at Ravensbrück concentration camp – as an officer. He asks whether she will take his hand as a sign of her forgiveness for all he represents. As he looks at her with his hand outstretched, she remembers him as one of the most violent guards of all. In her mind she sees him mocking her sister Betsie when she could no longer walk. Inside she cries out to God, 'I cannot forgive him!' Her beloved sister is dead and yet there he stands in front of her, wanting forgiveness.

Over several years of playing this scene, there were a couple of people in my life who I found it very difficult to forgive. The truth of playing this scene as Corrie, night after night, helped me to recognise that to forgive *is* to be free. At the end of the scene Corrie rages at Jesus and simply states, 'I cannot forgive this man, I can only raise my hand, I can do that much, you do the rest, Jesus.' She raises her hand to take the German officer's hand, and in doing so she is filled with a remarkable sense of grace and ends up saying, 'I forgive you brother, I forgive you with all of my heart.' What began as an almost perfunctory handshake, ends in a warm physical embrace. As I performed this, I would keep surrendering all my bitterness to God, so that my heart, like Corrie's, would stay free.

'To be a Christian means to forgive the inexcusable, because God has forgiven the inexcusable in you'.
C.S. Lewis, *The Weight of Glory*[10]

Forgiveness is really tough. How do we forgive the seemingly unforgiveable? In his book *Total Forgiveness*[11], R.T. Kendall reminds us that to forgive is to choose not to remember; we can't forget necessarily, but we can refuse to remember their sin against us. One truth that really helped me understand this further is that the Bible does not teach that what the person did was OK by Him, that it was alright for incredible wrongs and injustices to go unpunished, just that we can leave them with Him. Over the years as a pastor and as a person navigating pain along the way, I have seen the real importance of this. When we forgive even when people have not asked for our forgiveness, we simply declare that, with God's help, we will not let this cloud our future or hold us back in bitterness. It is both a single act and an ongoing process.

While we were researching for the adaptation of *The Hiding Place* from book to play, a few of us from Saltmine Trust went to meet some holocaust survivors at the National Holocaust Centre and Museum in Nottingham. We shared with a lady there the incredible story of Corrie ten Boom and the grace she found in

Christ to be able to forgive her persecutors. This lady, who was a survivor of the Auschwitz concentration camp, said with such deep pain in her eyes that she could never forgive and was still in prison in her heart. To me this is both understandable and incredibly sad. The writer of the Psalms knew how this felt, 'You have taken from me my closest friends and have made me repulsive to them. I am confined and I cannot escape; my eyes are dim with grief' (Psa. 88:8-9).

Jesus saw forgiveness as so vital to being one of His followers that He put it in the Lord's Prayer: 'Forgive us our debts, as we also have forgiven our debtors' (Matt. 6:12). It is when we fully appreciate our own need for forgiveness that we realise the importance to forgive others. By failing to forgive others, we imply that we accept Jesus' death for our own forgiveness, but we will still hold others to account for how they have hurt us.

'The quality of mercy is not strain'd, it droppeth as the gentle rain from heaven upon the place beneath... It blesseth him that gives and him that takes... It is an attribute to God himself; and earthly power doth then show likest God's when mercy seasons justice.' William Shakespeare, *The Merchant of Venice*

To help us understand the parable of the unforgiving servant in Matthew, Jesus uses the metaphor of debt collection and cancellation. In the parable, a servant is freed from a large debt and yet he will not release a fellow servant from a small amount. 'I cancelled all that debt of yours because you begged me to. Shouldn't you have had mercy on your fellow servant just as I had on you?' (Matt. 18:32-33).

So as we close this chapter, let us not listen to the lie or 'no' that we can't forgive, especially when it seems impossible, but remember Corrie ten Boom's example of the 'yes' and the freedom that comes when we forgive.

ELEVEN

Freed
to be
Loved

Occasionally, when I am speaking or performing at an event, I can find my attention drawn to the facial reactions of one particular person in a crowd. No matter how many other people are smiling and nodding in encouragement, the person I often 'see' most is the person who looks disengaged or even offended by what I am sharing. It was at one such speaking engagement that a lady seemed especially annoyed or upset by what I was saying. It was a weekend away attended by about two hundred women. The lady in question appeared most agitated when I talked about how much God loves us, and how He has a unique plan for each of us. She would either walk out or lower her head in a complete disagreement with anything spoken that suggested she had value.

'Shame corrodes the very part of us that believes we are capable of change.' Brene Brown[12]

Finally, on the last day, this lady came to see me in a state of real distress. She wanted me to know that she found any teaching on her value, or God's delight in her, very difficult to believe. She shared that, due to long-term abuse, it was inconceivable to her that she was worthy of anyone's love or anything that would make her appear lovable. In desperation we prayed to God, asking that she wouldn't leave the weekend without somehow knowing – once and for all, deep in the core of her being – that she was unconditionally loved. As I began to teach the final session, I was conscious of what we had prayed about, but also knew that the material I had prepared didn't seem especially relevant to her situation.

The event drew to a close, culminating in a beautiful Communion service and a time of ministry with the women that were there. In the crowded room, a young woman stood up. She was a student who during the worship had felt God asking her, 'What is your most precious possession, and would you be prepared to give it up for me?' She had decided that it was her watch, which, on the face, had a beautifully embossed dove made out of pearl. She looked around the room wondering who she might give it to and what to do next.

I watched in amazement as this young woman purposefully made her way towards the lady I had just been praying with, took off her watch, and gave it to her. As she did so she whispered, 'I don't know if this means anything, but I feel that God has asked me to tell you that this watch is the most valuable thing I own, but I should to give it to you because you are a treasured possession to Him.' Here was a young woman whose beautiful act of obedience was the absolute answer to a prayer she had no idea we had prayed, and for a woman whose name she didn't even know. For this lady, here was proof that God had used someone to show her once and for all that she was deeply loved. When Jesus Christ died for us, God sent His most treasured possession, His Son, to show us once and for all that we are loved, lovable, and forgiven.

'Do not conform to the pattern of this world, but be transformed by the renewing of your mind'
Romans 12:2

A few years later I was speaking at the Spring Harvest summer holiday in Le Pas Opton, France. On the very first evening, a lady came up to me and said, 'Judy, I'm not sure you remember me, but I had to come up and see you.' I looked into her warm, friendly face, searching my memory without success. I began to apologise just as she raised her arm – and there was the watch! The lovely lady wearing it was transformed inside and out. All the magazine makeovers could never have achieved what God's love had accomplished.

I love this story for two reasons. The first is because of the young student who was being part of the body of Christ at work. When we each play our part in the family of God, we can be the answer to someone else's heartfelt prayer. Prayer works – rarely in the way we had imagined, but it works! The second is the profound reminder that we can be transformed. This was only a part of one lady's journey of restoration but, nevertheless, it was a time when heaven touched earth with power to make a fundamental change, healing a deep-rooted pain with liberating truth.

Abuse is very closely linked to shame and to a completely underserved sense of worthlessness. The perpetrator of abuse often transfers the blame onto the victim themselves, so that they end up wearing it like a shroud of shame. Many victims of abuse feel a strong resistance to any gospel message that would say that they are beautiful, accepted or chosen. It is the completely opposite of all that they have learned to believe about themselves. Yet Jesus chose to align Himself with the broken, the shackled, the enslaved and the oppressed. He is the defender of the weak and the one who fights to set the captives free. Jesus brings life in all its fullness because of the Father's love.

When I became a Christian, a group of actors I was with were singing the hymn *Bread of Heaven*. As they sang 'my chains fell off my heart was free, I rose went forth and followed thee', something was released in me. It was a tangible, physical freedom. I knew that I was being set free.

The lie or the 'no' that the devil wants you to hear is that there is no hope or freedom. But the truth or 'yes' is that, 'if the Son sets you free, you will be free indeed' (John 8:36).

TWELVE

Hanging
on
UPSIDE DOWN

I was once participating in a leadership training course run by the Church Pastoral Aid Society. At the start of the first week of activities, we were given the warning that there would be times during the course when we would feel out of our comfort zones. However, they reassured us by explaining that, although we should expect to experience 'amber or red zone levels' in terms of fear or discomfort, should anything become 'ultraviolet zone level', we were to immediately ask to stop the activity. *Surely*, I thought to myself, *the Church Pastoral Aid Society will live up to their name and we can trust them to take good care of us.*

'Today's activity is abseiling!' the instructor announced on the second day. The plan was to climb up a nearby rock face and abseil down the other side. A man in our party called Roger was already emerging as the leader. He had a strong physique, had spent some time in the forces and seemed deeply self-assured and courageous. The fact that he was in our group was reassuring. My assessment of the challenge ahead was that the climb up the rock face would definitely be a red zone level for me, and anything beyond that would be ultraviolet. Using ropes, we climbed together as a group. Below, our reassuring pastoral aid leaders slowly diminished in size the higher we climbed; their encouraging words becoming harder to hear.

Eventually, having made it to the top with no real drama, we were rewarded with faint applause from those on the ground. However, as I stopped to consider our achievement so far, the reality of the next stage slowly dawned. We had to abseil down the other side of the cliff face; no other option was available. To shout 'ultraviolet' at this stage would have little or no effect in terms of getting me down. There was no alternative grassy knoll or gradual descent to roll down; abseiling over the precipice was the only route.

Roger was to go first, with me following. After some brief training in the art of staying upright and trusting in both the tension of the rope and the person guiding us from the top, we began our descent. Roger reassured me that he would cheer me on when it came to my turn.

Then the unthinkable happened. Halfway down the rock face, Roger swung upside down on his rope. Showing incredible levels of calmness and politeness, he shouted up to the young lad who was controlling his rope, 'What happens now?' To which came the response anyone in his position would dread: 'Not sure mate.'

Ultraviolet! This small boy (he seemed to be getting younger to me now) didn't have a clue what to do while Roger swung below, waiting for advice. The lad called across to another man called Chris, who was a seasoned climber. Within minutes, Chris had managed to right Roger and send him safely down the cliff to the welcome relief of our, now not fully trusted, pastoral aid team. 'Ultraviolet!' I shouted again inside, as I took my first step backwards off the cliff into the unknown. Chris the rescuer, sensing that I was still slightly traumatised by Roger's dramatic episode, agreed to abseil down beside me. This works very well for someone with my personality; I don't mind being pushed or even a little scared, as long as I know I'm not alone.

The episode ended with a very relieved group all making it down safely, but with a mild mistrust of our leaders from the Church Pastoral Aid Society. This, of course, turned out to be totally undeserved by the end of the week! Living as I do now in Birmingham, there has been little or no opportunity to continue to refine my abseiling skills, but I remain open to the possibility!

'For I am the LORD your God who takes hold of your right hand and says to you, Do not fear; I will help you' Isaiah 41:13

In the film *Superman*, there is a moment when Lois Lane is caught in midair by Superman and she cries out, 'You've got me, but who has got you?' There are times in our lives when we are hanging on by the skin of our teeth and we might ask the question, 'Who has got me?' At times we feel like shouting, 'What happens now?' We may have reached the point when we are swinging, hanging upside down at the end of our personal rope. One thing I am deeply convinced of is that we have a God who would never reply, 'Not sure mate!' We have a God who has control of our rope, and even when things seem upside-down He knows the way to right us, to redeem our descent and to catch our fall. The prophet Isaiah says this on behalf of God: 'For I am the LORD your God who takes hold of your right hand and says to you, Do not fear; I will help you' (Isa. 41:13).

God will never let go of us; in whatever storm or crisis we may find ourselves. He is present with us and able to rescue us when we call out to Him. God is trustworthy and His ways are just. He sent His Son Jesus to experience alongside us the climbs and the descents of life, to be a mouthpiece of instruction and to be God in human form. Taking a step of faith may seem like stepping backwards into the unknown, but we have God who never lets go of our rope, Jesus to advise us and the Holy Spirit to guide us every step of the way.

'Decide to trust Him for one little thing today, and before you know it, you'll find out He's so trustworthy you'll be putting your whole life in His hands.' Lyn Austin, *Candle in the Darkness*[13]

Jesus was in a boat with His friends when a storm hit them. The disciples feared for their lives and looked to Jesus for help, but He had fallen asleep. They must have asked this same question: 'Have you got us? Do you even care what happens to us? Are you about to let go of us?' They were so frightened that they woke up the sleeping Jesus. 'Lord, save us! We're going to drown!' (Matt. 8:25). Jesus response was to literally speak to the storm, to calm the sea that surrounds them. How is it possible that He could have slept through such a storm? It is because He knows that His Father, the creator and mastermind of all creation, has got us.

God speaks into the storms we face. He may not always calm the seas straightaway, but He has promised never to leave us, even when we feel like He is asleep. We may believe the 'no' that we have no one to trust with our life, but the truth or 'yes' is that He is holding our rope, and He is not going to let go of us.

THIRTEEN

Two
Sides
of the
Story

It had been a really good Christmas visiting family and friends in London. I always love the opportunity Christmas offers to gather us around my sister's table, one of my happiest places to be. Over a few glasses of mulled wine and mince pies, we swap presents. One particular gift had been a real encouragement to me. A close friend, Lizzie, had given me the word 'live' in white wood set on a free standing plinth. What a brilliant reminder to live life to the full; to remember that Jesus said, 'I have come that they may have life, and have it to the full' (John 10:10).

On my return home, I proudly displayed the gift in my bay window facing inwards, next to the Christmas tree, as a reminder to live. At New Year, my friend John dropped by to visit. Coming in through the door, he immediately asked me if I was OK and if Christmas had been alright. He seemed concerned, so I assured him it had been a lovely time. 'Oh,' he replied, 'it's just that you've got "evil" displayed in your window.' What looked like from the inside a tangible reminder of God's goodness, from the outside appeared to wish evil upon all who passed by. Not a great message for a church pastor! I quickly moved the sign to another spot where it could only be read one way!

There will always be two views on the world, two ways of looking at a situation, two ways to live. In Luke 23 we read how two criminals hung either side of Jesus Christ on the cross. One criminal compared his own life in shame with the innocent Saviour dying beside him. He cried out to Jesus for forgiveness, and was told that paradise would be his destiny that very day. The other, dying beside the same innocent Jesus, had the same opportunity to cry out, but his only cries were those that mocked Jesus.

'Convicted by the same system, condemned to the same death, surrounded by the same crowd, equally close to the same Jesus, beginning with the same sarcasm, but only one man changed... One good choice for eternity offsets a thousand bad on earth.' Max Lucado, *He Chose the Nails*[14]

We have a choice as to which 'thief' we will be. Will we live our lives as if this earth is all there is, and take the punishment we deserve? Or will we cry out to Jesus, 'remember me when you come into your kingdom' (Luke 23:42)? The thief is one person we know for certain is in heaven with God. This means there is hope for everyone who says that they are truly sorry to God. All of us have made a mess of things at some stage. All of us have fallen short of God's standards.

The life of Joseph begins as a series of lows including family betrayal, abandonment in a pit, false accusations and prison, but ends on a high with him in a palace as

Prime Minister of Egypt. At the end of the story, Joseph says to his brothers, 'You intended to harm me, but God intended it for good' (Gen. 50:20). God has the last word in Joseph's story, and I believe He has the last word in each of our stories too. He is the one who overcomes evil with good.

'You intended to harm me, but God intended it for good' Genesis 50:20

Reading Philip Yancey's book, *What's So Amazing About Grace?*, was very helpful for my mother and enabled her to finally 'cross the line' and become a Christian. So it was incredible that a year later, I was able to meet and get to know Philip and his wife, Janet. For several years we, at Saltmine Trust, toured with them, dramatising many different aspects of Philip's brilliant books. During one tour of South Africa we visited Pollsmoor Prison in Cape Town, which was once described as the most evil place in the whole of Africa.

Some years earlier a woman from Johannesburg, called Joanna, had heard on her radio that there were 279 violent attacks in the prison that year, and in response, she wanted to do something to show God's peace and love. So with the permission of the prison governor, Joanna travelled to Cape Town to start Bible study sessions with the inmates. By the time we visited, some of the men had become committed Christians. In one cell, there were 50 huge men sharing a cell designed for 30, which meant having to top and tail bunk beds and even sleep on the floor. Scrawled on the walls, however, were Bible verses and encouragements learnt from Joanna during their studies. One read, 'Surely the presence of the Lord is in this place.' Something transformational was happening in this prison – a woman had answered the call of Jesus to share His love in a place where love was evidently absent! We sang with murderers, gang members and rapists overwhelmed by the forgiveness of Jesus. Their joy and faith was both contagious and inspiring.

'In some ways, evil is backhanded proof of God's existence' Philip Yancey[15]

After one year of Joanna sharing the Bible with increasing numbers of inmates, statistics showed that a miracle had taken place. There had been just two assaults that year – from 279 to just two! The truth and light of Jesus had turned men from the darkness to light, from evil to goodness. When interviewed in a BBC documentary, Joanna was asked, 'How did you, a woman from the townships of Johannesburg, bring God to the most evil place in Africa?' Her reply was beautiful. 'Oh, I didn't bring Him here, I just made Him visible.'

The light shines in the darkness, and the light in one woman's heart had changed a whole community. Joanna lived by the truth of the book of Romans: 'Do not be overcome by evil, but overcome evil with good' (Rom. 12:21). That evil is winning is a 'no', because the 'yes' is that God has already won.

Dear Reader,

I hope and pray that each of these stories have encouraged and challenged you in some way. May you be blessed in the discovery that there is incredible hope for you as the `yes' of God impacts your life.

If you have read this book as someone who is curious but unconvinced about the Christian faith, I would highly recommend trying an Alpha course near to where you live (search for alpha.org/try). Alpha is an informal series of sessions that explore the basics of the Christian faith and provides an opportunity to ask questions. Alternatively, pop into a church where there are people who can continue your faith journey with you.

God loves you and me so implicitly that He died for us. In my view, that makes Him well worth living for.

Have a wonderful time as you explore your new name and identity shaped by the incredible love and grace of God!

Judy

Endnotes

[1] Timothy Keller, *The Reason for God* (London: Hodder and Stoughton, 2009)

[2] 'Tripping Over Joy' from *I Heard God Laughing: Renderings of Hafiz* by Daniel Ladinsky (New York: Penguin Books, 2006)

[3] W.H. Auden, *Collected Poems* (London: Faber & Faber, 2004)

[4] THE SCREWTAPE LETTERS by C.S. Lewis © C.S. Lewis Pte Ltd. 1942. Used with permission.

[5] Sylvia Nasar, *A Beautiful Mind* (London: Faber & Faber, 2002)

[6] Hymn by Anna L. Waring, *In Heavenly Love Abiding*, 1850

[7] Ted Loder, extract from 'Come now to find us', *My Heart in My Mouth* (Wipf and Stock, 2013).

[8] Anne Frank, *The Diary of a Young Girl* (London: Puffin, 2007)

[9] Corrie ten Boom, *The Hiding Place* (London: Hodder & Stoughton, 2004)

[10] THE WEIGHT OF GLORY by C.S. Lewis © C.S. Lewis Pte Ltd. 1949. Used with permission.

[11] R.T. Kendall, *Total Forgiveness* (Lake Mary, FL: Charisma House, 2007)

[12] Brene Brown, *I Thought It Was Just Me* (New York: Penguin Putnam, 2008)

[13] Lyn Austin, *Candle in the Darkness* (Minneapolis, MN: Bethany House Publishers, 2014)

[14] Max Lucado, *He Chose the Nails* (Nashville, TN: Thomas Nelson, 2017)

[15] Cited by Philip Yancey in *Rumors of Another World* (Grand Rapids, MI: Zondervan, 2003)

With special thanks to:

The Fullbrook family for providing a lovely Devon space for me to write, and especially Leanne, whose sketches of dogs were an initial inspiration!

Erin and Paul, my writing buddies and Helen, Jim and the girls for the writing space in Croatia.

Sharon, Val and Caroline for initially proofreading the book.

Andy, Tim and Riverside Church, Birmingham for their love, encouragement and prayers.

Adrian Plass for writing the wonderful foreword and to Jeff Lucas and Amy Boucher Pye for their kind words and recommendations.

Andrea Bodle, my lovely, ever-patient and brilliant editor. Joanna Duke for her wonderful work on the design of the book.

Lynette Brooks for catching the vision and taking the risk, and to the whole CWR team, who have made this such an enjoyable experience.

Transforming lives

CWR's vision is to enable people to experience personal transformation through applying God's Word to their lives and relationships.

Our Bible-based training and resources help people around the world to:
• Grow in their walk with God
• Understand and apply Scripture to their lives
• Resource themselves and their church
• Develop pastoral care and counselling skills
• Train for leadership
• Strengthen relationships, marriage and family life and much more.

Our insightful writers provide daily Bible reading notes and other resources for all ages, and our experienced course designers and presenters have gained an international reputation for excellence and effectiveness.

CWR's Training and Conference Centre in Surrey, England, provides excellent facilities in idyllic settings – ideal for both learning and spiritual refreshment.

CWR Applying God's Word
to everyday life and relationships

CWR, Waverley Abbey House,
Waverley Lane, Farnham,
Surrey GU9 8EP, UK

Telephone: **+44 (0)1252 784700**
Email: **info@cwr.org.uk**
Website: **www.cwr.org.uk**

Registered Charity No. 294387
Company Registration No. 1990308